John E. R
Suanne D

HIGH STAKES, HIGH PERFORMANCE

Making Remedial Education Work

COMMUNITY COLLEGE PRESS®
a division of the
American Association of Community Colleges
Washington, D.C.

The American Association of Community Colleges (AACC) is the primary advocacy organization for the nation's community colleges. The association represents 1,100 two-year, associate degree-granting institutions and some 10 million students. AACC provides leadership and service in five key areas: legislative advocacy; monitoring of national issues and trends; collection, analysis, and dissemination of information; representation with other educational agencies and the national media; and research and publication of news and scholarly analysis.

Requests for permission should be sent to
Community College Press
American Association of Community Colleges
One Dupont Circle, NW
Suite 410
Washington, DC 20036
Fax: (202) 223-9390

Printed in the United States of America.

ISBN 0-87117-321-2

I am increasingly impatient with people who ask whether a student is "college material." We are not building a college with a student. The question we ought to ask is whether the college is . . . student material. It is the student we are building, and it is the function of the college to facilitate that process. We have him as he is, rather than as we wish he were. . . . We are still calling for much more change in the student than we are in the faculty. . . . Can we come up with the professional attitudes [necessary to] put us in the business of tapping pools of human talent not yet touched? . . . The greatest challenge facing the community college is to make good on the promise of the open door.

—Edmund J. Gleazer Jr., 1970

Contents

Preface

The American Association of Community Colleges commissioned this study of remedial education in community colleges as a framework for describing context, generating discussion, and encouraging action. Always controversial, remedial education is a multifaceted issue that we have worked with and researched for more than 30 years. The public's and the academy's interest in this aspect of the community college curriculum—what some have called the fulcrum that balances colleges' commitment to excellence with student access and success—has waxed and waned during these years. During the last five years, however, there has been a heightened interest in remedial education—what it is, who provides it, how much it costs, how it is evaluated, and where it belongs.

The questions come from within the higher education community as well as from policymakers, the media, and the general public. This interest is neither subtle nor mild-mannered; rather, it is critical, angry, and hostile. It is turning action into law; into legislative debate, bills, and statutes; and into evaluative queries, charges, and mandates by individuals and groups who have a history of making change happen. Cases in point include the South Carolina statute prohibiting remedial education in universities and giving total responsibility for remedial education to community colleges; the Florida statute placing limits on time and funding, mandating assessment and "compensatory education"; and the new federal Government Performance and Results Act (GPRA), guaranteed to change the way community colleges applying for federal money must describe their results. Soon there will be other compelling reasons for community colleges to consider how they will match efforts to results and results to promises. For now, we have attempted to organize the most current information to help focus discussion and remind readers of older issues that have never been more important.

A note about terminology: Historically, the terms *remedial* and *developmental* have been used interchangeably to label preparatory programs or courses of study that have as their central purpose the development of basic skills to such levels that students can enroll in and profit from instruction in regular college-credit courses. In practice, however, many educators make a distinction between the two terms, using *developmental* to describe instruction that prepares students for specific college courses or programs (e.g., studying effectively, thinking critically), and *remedial* to describe instruction that has or should have been provided in the past (e.g., reading, math, writing). Remedial education has evolved from detached efforts to rectify individual skill deficiencies to more complex, organized efforts to develop the cognitive and affective talents that describe the whole student. This movement away from traditional ideas about remediation and toward a more developmental response is a critical feature of this report and in the descriptions of college efforts. The programs we feature link real-life activities with new learning and meet other academic needs, for example, by teaching study skills that increase learning. The more widely used term among educators is *developmental education;* we applaud the attitudes and beliefs that it reflects.

We have chosen to use *remedial education* here, however. It is the term that speaks directly to the current issue of meeting the challenges of academic underpreparedness with strategies that work. The term has acquired considerable negative overtones from decades of arguments about appropriateness and quality, but it is convenient because it requires little explanation. Moreover, the general public, policymakers, and the media typically refer to remedial, rather than to developmental, education, and we must pay close attention to these constituencies, which will ask so many of the critical questions that drive future action.

In preparing this framework, we reviewed current research about open-door policies; underprepared students; faculty; and remedial education programs, including their objectives and evaluation practices. Included are findings from an abbreviated survey we conducted during the writing of this report, in which we spoke or corresponded with representatives of selected community colleges with reputations for successful remedial programs. We also reviewed descriptions of more than 30 other programs, analyzing their efforts to succeed with the at-risk student population.

We concluded this study by reviewing some key issues about which colleges should be informed, and we made recommendations for initiating, developing, and improving current practice. Although the work is intentionally brief, we endeavored to describe accurately the tone and major themes surrounding remediation in community colleges. We also gathered what we consider to be a balanced array of secondary sources that readers may wish to consult for further insight into the remediation debate.

John E. Roueche
Suanne D. Roueche
The University of Texas at Austin

Chapter 1

Rocks and Hard Places: Identifying the Problems

More than five years ago, we argued that changing demographics, burgeoning technologies, and a faltering public education system have the United States caught somewhere between a rock and a hard place. Nothing has occurred in the interim to change our minds. Socially, demographically, and economically, the United States has its hands full with persistent problems that loom even larger when we consider that the efforts to combat the increase of illiteracy, unemployment, welfare dependency, racial tensions, crime, and other social ills have had few overwhelmingly successful results.

As "democracy's colleges" and "America's social inventions," community colleges may be the best institutions of higher education to develop viable responses to many of the country's problems. However, successful responses to these problems could escape our grasp unless we move beyond simplistic explanations of the problems to an understanding of their complexity. The problems that we can describe only broadly here may help explain the challenges brought to community colleges by ever-larger numbers of underprepared students.

Illiteracy is widespread in America. There is no common definition for literacy, and various agencies use their own, ranging from the less-dependable attendance in school and grade-level definitions to the more practical indicators of performance on reading tasks. Studies of schooling in the 1950s generated suspicions that remaining in school did not necessarily increase one's chances of becoming more literate; unfortunately, studies in the 1980s and 1990s confirmed those suspicions (Roueche and Roueche 1993). A 1975 study conducted at the University of Texas at Austin, using the task approach, placed the number of American adults who were not functionally literate at 1 in 5, or 20 percent (Northcutt, et al., 1975). In sum, large numbers of people living in the United States cannot perform such everyday tasks as reading bus schedules or determining the correct change for even small purchases.

Growing demand for workers who can communicate, perform simple mathematical procedures, and think critically puts a high number of people at risk for being out of work. Of special concern are recent studies that indicate that more than 25 percent of the U.S. workforce is functionally illiterate. Our adult population is now and will grow more underprepared for work and, therefore, will require more education, more skills, more adaptability, and more collaboration among its workers (Brock 1993).

There are few unskilled jobs left, and the majority of new jobs require a high school diploma and some postsecondary education. Gaps between skilled and unskilled jobs and workers are widening at a rapid pace. Almost 96 percent of manufacturing firms responding to a recent survey indicated that they provide some education and training for their hourly employees. At least two-thirds indicated they provide remedial instruction in reading, writing, math, and problem solving, and additional instruction in such basic work skills as arriving at work on time and collaborating to solve workplace problems (National Association of Manufacturers 1997).

New and evolving technologies drive the demand for workers with some experience or training at basic technological levels; the computer is now so common a tool that almost all businesses use its most basic applications, even in jobs that require no education beyond high school. Almost half of all workers report that as job skills change, they are required to get more training to keep the jobs they have (National Center for Education Statistics [hereafter cited as NCES] 1996). Adults will respond to these increasing job demands by returning to college for further education or to prepare for different jobs. As a result, colleges will continue to be faced with increasingly diverse student populations.

Studies have demonstrated that members of the general public do not adequately understand the "skills gap" phenomenon; they can articulate little about the relationship between work and education and have little understanding of what experts on both sides of the issue believe. Most people do not see any connection between the country's economic health and the skills of its workforce. Most believe that motivation, not skill, is the key to getting a job. Most believe that menial jobs are available for anyone who wants to work and will make the effort to find them. And people universally believe that the problem is too few jobs, not too few people who can do them (Immerwahr et al. 1991).

Major changes in U.S. demographics are occurring at the same time as our greatest need for an educated citizenry. If trends continue, more young people than ever before will reach adulthood without the skills and knowledge they need to be gainfully employed. As these individuals are preparing for and entering the workplace, increasing numbers of today's workers are thinking about retirement. Our population is aging—by 2030 there will be more than 69.3 million persons over the age of 65 (more than are under 18), up from 33.5 million in 1995 (Preston 1996). The future of our Social Security system is a commonly discussed challenge that this aging population will face, as the number of workers available to support each retiree declines. Today, approximately 3.4 workers support each retiree, but if trends continue, by 2020 only 2.0 workers per retiree will be available. Adding to concerns about the threat to the Social Security system are serious concerns about worker preparedness for skilled jobs.

The population of the United States is becoming more diverse. Trends indicate that in fewer than 20 years, non-Hispanic whites will make up less than half the total population. Historical data link minority groups to educational underpreparedness, with strong links to less-than-adequate facilities in the schools that serve them and the communities in which they live. "Today, almost a third of African Americans and half of all Hispanics have no high school diploma, and more than four-fifths of these growing populations have no postsecondary degree" (McCabe and Day 1998, 15). And while participation in higher education has increased for 18- to 24-year-olds in all income groups in the last 30 years, the gaps between high and low income levels and college completion rates have not changed (Hartle and King 1997). As various states struggle to change these trends, they seek to encourage participation and graduation by more low-income students. For example, state budgets may include funding incentives for colleges that enroll and retain economically disadvantaged students.

Both immigration and Hispanic birthrates are increasing the U.S. population. Immigration is up by more than 50 percent in the last decade, primarily as a result of immigration from Latin America and Asia, and increasingly as a result of immigration from the Middle East (Hodgkinson 1997). Illegal immigrants from the Third World, perhaps more than five million to date, already live in the United States; the largest numbers of legal and illegal immigrants continue to arrive from

Mexico, up to 52 percent of all immigrants in 1991, and climbing about 8 percent each year since 1989 (Fallon 1996).

In the early 1900s, unskilled immigrants were accommodated as manpower for relatively unskilled work; today less than 25 percent of all jobs could be classified as unskilled. These are typically dead-end jobs in the low-paying service sector (Boyle 1990). Moreover, while the overwhelming majority of new immigrants are unprepared to enter today's skilled workforce, with training they have the potential to reverse the shortfalls that will occur in the workforce as the result of increasing retirements among "baby boomers."

Poverty and undereducation are inextricably linked to each other as well as to decaying neighborhoods, crime, unemployment, welfare, hopelessness, and cynicism. The numbers of children born into poverty continue to escalate—in 1990, at least 1 in every 5 American children was born into poverty, and children have been referred to as the poorest segment of our society (National Center on Education and the Economy 1990). Texas governor George W. Bush announced in campaigns for educational reform that 1 in 3 Texas children are born out of wedlock, a prescription for poverty and undereducation. Even this dismal situation does not totally prepare us for the news that poverty rates in the United States are "among the highest in the developed world" (Hodgkinson 1997, 7).

The consequences of poverty are enormous. Uneducated adults, unable to provide for their families, will create another generation of children who lack sufficient care in the womb to avoid gross learning disabilities, who receive insufficient stimulation during the three years after birth when care and nurturing are most critical to normal development, and who have limited social interaction with homes and community cultures that understand that literacy is essential for a child's readiness on the first day of school (Stitcht and McDonald 1990). Public school officials continue to decry the increasing numbers of children who enter the first grade so far behind emotionally, socially, and cognitively that they have little chance of catching up. A generation of undereducated adults creates a generation of school dropouts, who are the next generation of undereducated adults.

Although national reform policies are shrinking the number of welfare recipients and achieving some encouraging success, many critics point out that moving individuals off welfare rolls and into low-paying, low-skill jobs does not move them out of poverty. The majority of welfare recipients are so academically underprepared, so lacking in work experience, so poor, and so unaware of the relationships between work and education, that they must be educated about the most basic skills before they can consider enrolling, much less being successful, in postsecondary education. Many critics also warn that current welfare policies that put work before education hold little promise for recipients' opportunities for upward mobility.

On average, almost 50 percent of all first-time community college students test as underprepared for the academic demands of college-level courses and programs and are advised to enroll in at least one remedial class. This percentage of underprepared students has not changed significantly across the United States in at least two decades, and there is no evidence that it will be reduced in the near future, although in individual states percentages have fluctuated.

First-time community college students are a diverse group, but the large number of recent high school graduates among the unprepared students in this mix is an obvious indictment of our educational system. Moreover, high school graduates who do not enroll in college immediately after leaving high school are more likely to need remediation in more than one subject area than graduates who enroll immediately. Researchers warn that although high school graduates may have taken the correct number of courses to complete their secondary education, more often than not they are not the right courses for pursuing postsecondary work (Horn, Chen, and MPR Associates 1998). Although almost half of all high school graduates complete a college preparatory curriculum (four years of English and three years each of math, science, and social studies) (Hartle and King 1997), there is ample evidence that concerns about the quality of the instruction are justified.

Higher education has not demonstrated any quick fixes to the problems that lead to underpreparedness. There is some comfort in the thought that had there been any quick solutions, American ingenuity would have ferreted them out and implemented them by now. That could be one argument—fixing just takes time, and we are way down the road with implementation. Another could be that we have been overwhelmed, underestimating the complexities; and while we are not very far down the road, we are working to get there.

Some colleges are well prepared to make these arguments and provide evidence to support their positions. Most have believed that the problems would somehow resolve themselves, or that somebody else would resolve them. There is little evidence that the majority of community colleges have a solid grasp of the extent of the problems, much less have designed and implemented responses that the public and the politics of the day will continue to accept.

The current trend toward accountability indicates that politicians and the public believe that most college responses to student underpreparedness consist of poorly designed performance measures against shortsighted standards. Some states have argued for and some have won the authority to give community colleges full responsibility for educating underprepared students. There is no evidence that they have done so because they believe without a doubt that our colleges are the last best places for remedial education to occur; in fact, many legislators have observed that results of remediation at all levels are dismal.

The proposition that remediation should be eliminated from four-year college and university curricula, as one effort to maintain the perceived traditionally high standards at these institutions, has garnered increased support. The arguments about remediation providers and policies, and the laws that are being written to evaluate more carefully the results of college remediation endeavors, indicate that community colleges must take more seriously their efforts to document the effectiveness of these programs.

Chapter 2

Remedial Education: The Balancing Act for Access and Excellence

Setting the Remediation Context

Remediation in higher education is a multifaceted problem. Critics argue *against* remediation at four-year colleges and universities, *for* remediation on community college campuses only, *against* remedial courses in community colleges, *for* remediation only in the public schools where the need for it should have been prevented in the first place, and *against* individuals who may have thrown away earlier opportunities. Social, demographic, and educational factors will swell the population of underprepared students entering higher education for at least the next two decades. Unconscionable numbers of high school graduates underprepared for college work are but one segment of the underprepared population; they are joined by high school dropouts, GED recipients, returning adults, new immigrants, welfare recipients, and others. These students will represent ever-larger proportions of every new freshman community college class.

Remedial education's multifaceted nature explains, in part, the enormous array of responses that community colleges make to it. The only common pattern we can identify among community colleges is that they all offer remedial courses (NCES 1996). Common criticisms have focused on poor performance of remedial programs, dead-end opportunities for at-risk students, duplication of effort, and doubling of expenditures.

The majority of current remediation efforts in higher education are perceived as inefficient and ineffective. Unfortunately, many of the criticisms are valid. Moreover, they are leading to actions that in the near future will require community colleges to respond to questions that few have asked themselves and that most are unprepared or unwilling to answer. Asking the right questions is one place to begin, and we have never had more reasons to do so than now.

Not a New Phenomenon

Higher education has a long tradition of remediation; even in earlier, more homogeneous populations of college freshmen, some students needed special attention before tackling the rigors of their chosen disciplines. However, as student populations became more heterogeneous with more relaxed access to higher education, increasing numbers of students were underprepared in one or more of the most basic reading, writing, and mathematics skills—so underprepared that they had little chance of survival in college-level courses. Early on, community colleges enrolled these students in remedial programs in order to develop their skills to the levels required for college-level work, then sent them on their way.

Over time, it became clear that these efforts were inadequate and shortsighted. Students were rarely better off for the remediation. Most became early casualties of the remedial effort or of regular academic courses; in a few short years, it became apparent that this approach was too simplistic for such a complex problem. If remediation was to be the vehicle by which underprepared students would have access to higher education, and if it was to have a future in the community college curriculum, the colleges had to determine what students were going to learn in these remedial programs and how the learning could be evaluated.

A 1968 study found that most remedial programs in community colleges were poorly conceptualized and poorly performed. In 1971, we were warned that remediation was a "high-risk" activity for the "new" student in higher education (Cross 1971). Without a doubt, it was high risk for colleges, which received poor marks for their remedial efforts, and which were censured for their "revolving doors" and their "cooling out" practices (Roueche and Roueche 1993).

While the problem of underpreparation has not been unique to community colleges, there is ample evidence to support the argument that considerably more risk factors are associated with students who come to community colleges than with students who go elsewhere. Unlike other institutions of higher education, community colleges have extended an invitation in the spirit and language of the "open door" and laid out the welcome mat to a highly diverse population; community colleges are obligated on principle and funded by law to match the abilities of underprepared students in their curriculum and instruction, and to give those students true access to higher education.

Given that remediation in higher education has received such enormous criticism for decades, both in and out of the academy, it is amazing that for the most part it has escaped substantively intrusive policies and mandates for change. Until the very recent past, all the criticisms and policies have had little effect.

Community colleges are becoming sites for the latest war on remedial education. The voices of the critics who have called loud and long for higher education to justify, reform, or abolish remedial education are no longer out of sync or out of tune; they are now speaking in one voice. Remediation in higher education is being systematically and effectively dismantled by politicians responding to their own and their constituents' concerns and demands.

The Open Door: Resolving the Question of Access

The first major study of remedial education in community colleges did not recommend closing the open door, but the study's findings did trigger a prophetic warning by John Lombardi, then the assistant superintendent of the Los Angeles City School Districts: "Unless solutions are found, it [education of the underprepared student] will become as serious for junior colleges as it is now for the elementary and secondary schools" (Roueche 1968, vi). And so it has.

If control resides where support originates, community colleges must meet community needs. The great community college experiment in providing extended educational opportunities for all was founded on the notion that an educated citizenry is essential to our nation's well-being. As an American social invention (Gleazer 1963), the community college was to offer postsecondary programs that would match a wide spectrum of community needs and relate economically and efficiently to the total pattern of educational opportunity (Wattenbarger and Godwin 1962).

The concept of the open door is unique to community colleges. It was established on the belief that education is necessary for the maintenance of the democracy, is essential for the improvement of society, and helps equalize opportunity for all people (Roueche 1968). The open door, early on, was the embodiment of that belief and the symbol of community colleges' efforts to live up to their reputation as democracy's colleges. Community colleges have claimed full bragging rights to the great promise and potential of the open door, and have defended it against critics—both in and out of the academy—who have argued for closing it.

While the lure of this great promise is understandable, *open-door* policies have put community colleges in danger of losing public trust. The term *open door* appeals to a broad audience, it is easy to understand, and it is identified with community colleges (Vaughan 1985). But there are serious misconceptions about what the open door allows. Not a carte blanche invitation to enroll in any program area, the open door is, rather, access to instruction from which the student can profit.

Of all the issues surrounding remedial education, it is the lack of agreement about its definition that leads to the most criticism. The open door does not give students who meet general admission requirements the option of enrolling in any program or curriculum area they wish; rather, their choices are limited by the academic skills they possess and the prerequisites they have mastered.

One researcher has described a student's experience thus: A student meets the general admission requirements, receives a key, and walks through the open door. But the keys are not alike; instead, the student's skills and experiences are represented on this key by grooves and notches that will unlock some doors and not others. For example, the key will not open the liberal arts door if the key's notches and grooves do not match those (that is, prerequisite coursework or skills) on the lock to the liberal arts door. However, all of the keys do have the appropriate notches and grooves to open the doors to areas where academic help is available—for example, the door to guidance and counseling, or the door to developmental education where the student "can get those prerequisites added to the key" (Vaughan 1985, 21–22).

The few common elements among their institutional policies, programs, and practices signal that community colleges would be hard pressed to articulate a common definition of the open door. The history of the open door is full of supporters and critics of the expenditures of time, effort, and money required to address the challenges created by student diversity. We choose to move forward on the assumption that community colleges have agreed that the open door obligates each college, within its limits, to pursue the overarching mission of providing educational opportunities, matching diverse skills and abilities with curriculum.

What happens between the underprepared student and the postsecondary institution is of such importance that it has perpetuated a simmering controversy for at least three decades. We can address here but a few of the issues that have brought this controversy to a rolling boil.

Just beyond the Open Door

Why is there no agreement among community colleges about the role they should play in remedial education? Increasingly, there have been heated debates about whether remedial education is justified in higher education. The most contentious issue is whether community colleges should be the sole providers of remedial education. The consensus of the more vocal debaters is that remedial curricula are neither appropriate nor legitimate in any upper-level institutions including community colleges and that efforts to remove remediation courses and programs from their curricula should begin immediately.

On the other hand, a number of states are now considering placing all remediation efforts in their community colleges, eliminating and prohibiting remediation at four-year colleges and universities. Some states have already established policies to that end. In Florida, Missouri, and South Carolina, for example, all remedial courses and programs have been banned from state four-year colleges and universities. Legislative discussion and strong political support for implementation are striking evidence that similar state-mandated policies are in the immediate futures of California, Georgia, Massachusetts, New York (the CUNY system in New York), Texas, and Virginia, and, most likely, a number of other states.

Even in community colleges that have promised access to higher education and have extended an invitation to broadly heterogeneous communities, critics of remedial education argue that at-risk students pose too much of a risk for the institution—that their very presence would damage a college's reputation for providing quality education—and that limited funds are more wisely spent on students who are better prepared and more likely to succeed in more rigorous college-level work.

There are also those who, consciously or not, are affected by "the importance of being smart" (Astin 1998, 12). For these educators, teaching at-risk students poses a problem: If it is believed that those who teach smart students are themselves smart, those who teach less-smart students might themselves be thought less able. In the final analysis, these educators "value *being* smart much more than . . . *developing* smartness"

(Astin 1998, 12), a position that is antithetical to the community college mission—and, arguably, to the mission of all higher education.

Who is to blame, who should pay, and why should we pay again? Some critics blame public education: Community college trustees, legislators, and taxpayers ask why colleges should provide remedial work to high school graduates who should have developed basic skills at the secondary level. In 1995, in Maryland, when more than 46,000 entering freshmen were not ready for college-level work, one trustee was appalled that 4,700 of these unprepared freshmen enrolled in his community college when the full- and part-time students totaled only 20,350. Some state legislatures, such as those in Montana and West Virginia, have discussed requiring public school districts to pay for remedial courses that their graduates must take when they enroll in college (Locksley 1998).

Some critics blame students: They should have been more responsible and taken college-preparatory courses in high school; if they must retake a remedial college course, students should be assessed as much as twice the regular credit-hour fee. One community college trustee observed that it is more difficult to support the idea of providing basic skill instruction for recent high school graduates than for students who have been out of the classroom a long time. Another commented that one college effort to remediate the problem is bad enough, but that second and third efforts are too many. His solution was to cover the cost at state expense on the first try, assess the student 50 percent of the cost on the second, assess full tuition on the third, and not allow a fourth try (Locksley 1998).

Other solutions are products of similar persuasions. By state statute, each Florida community college must conduct mandatory testing with the same instrument (a test prepared under contract with the state), and students must complete all preparatory courses (Florida community colleges' legal title for remedial courses and programs) indicated by the test results (in a sequence to be decided). Students pay for their first college preparatory course at the same per-credit-hour rate assessed for a college-credit course. Students who fail their first attempt must repeat the preparatory course, but for second and subsequent attempts must pay for instruction at out-of-state tuition rates, unless the student declares a financial hardship and the additional charge is waived. A repeated attempt costs almost four times the regular per-credit-hour fee.

Some lawmakers challenge the wisdom of providing financial aid to students who are enrolled in remedial courses—commonly referred to as ability to benefit—arguing that by eliminating financial aid to these students there would be more funds available to provide increased aid to "more qualified students." According to a 1997 report published by the General Accounting Office,

> Some members of the Congress seek to improve targeting of Title IV funds by restricting the use of financial aid to postsecondary education courses. In speculating that a large percentage of students receiving financial aid use it to pay for remedial courses, these members want to eliminate the financial aid awarded to students needing such courses and reallocate it to more qualified students. According to these members, the Congress could materially augment or enhance the financial aid packages of students remaining eligible for Title IV funding without providing additional appropriations. (Blanchette 1997, 1)

Lawmakers complain that in giving federal aid to these students, taxpayers have actually paid twice to educate them. It is a compelling argument, but not necessarily accurate: Many first-time freshmen, in some community colleges as many as half, did not cost taxpayers the first time. They do not hold high school diplomas or GED certificates, or they are immigrants and English is not their first language, and so on. A majority of first-time freshmen are considerably older than 18 and have not been in a classroom in a long time; they don't have the skills they need to succeed at college-level work without intervention. Finally, only about half of high school graduates go on to college and only about 25 percent of remedial education students are recent high school graduates. Not all high school graduates are college-ready; less than half take college-preparatory courses, and many of those will need some remediation before taking college-level courses. Although the argument is basically unsound, it continues to support criticisms that community colleges could help to diffuse by sharing demographic information with lawmakers and the public.

Critics also blame community colleges themselves: They should have been more demanding of public education, more vocal about poorly performing graduates, and more collaborative in working with schools to solve the problem early on. By offering remedial education, colleges hold out an alternative to high school students who would prefer to play now and pay later. The critics argue that community colleges and four-year colleges and universities "should increasingly assume that more advanced learning occurs during high school than has in the past—and educate accordingly" (Reising 1997, 172); that "access" must yield to "achievement" and colleges must "start requiring admissions committees to actually insist on some capacity to do college-level work" (Moloney 1996, 11A); and that "higher education [must] share blame for the pervasive decline of standards and accountability . . . Continuing the system of free passes does no one any favor, it only debases . . . American public education" (Moloney 1996, 11A).

With increased demands for colleges to document and evaluate their performance, is remedial education too high risk? More than half of all students in higher education are enrolled in community colleges, and if predictions for the next three to five years come true, the numbers will increase wildly. Enrollments in higher education are projected to increase from an estimated 13.9 million in 1995 to 16.1 million by 2007 or 20 million by 2010, and " 'traditional' is a word that not often will apply" (McClenney 1998, 1). The greater numbers will be accompanied by an even greater range of characteristics—from the more familiar first-generation or first-time college students who are beginning the postsecondary experience woefully underprepared in basic skills, to the relatively new population of students who have earned four-year degrees but are coming to upgrade their skills or prepare for a specific technical degree. In many community colleges, the latter group represents fully one-fourth of all incoming students (Milliron and Leach 1998). The efforts required to serve such diversity, especially as college resources continue to decline, will further fuel arguments between those who support closing the open door and those who fight for the egalitarian tradition of keeping it open.

The National Center for Education Statistics' 1996 report indicates that more than three-quarters of all students taking remedial courses passed them with a C or better; however, passing rates at community colleges were lower than those in other institutions by between 5 and 15 points. Fewer full-time, first-time freshmen who took one or more remedial courses were likely to return the following fall semester. Data about how well all students who successfully complete their remedial courses fare in college-level work are encouraging (NCES 1995); however, attrition data from remedial courses are not. Regardless of some good news, the public perception is that remedial courses are not necessarily successful.

> Will community colleges continue to offer their students a pathway to the bachelor's degree, or will they function primarily at the bottom rung of an ever-stricter two-track system of higher education? Will those disadvantaged students who are tracked into the growing maze of remediation in the community college sector ever transfer to four-year institutions? (Shaw 1997, 295)

What would assuming full responsibility for remediation in higher education mean for community colleges? With but a few states taking serious action in this direction, it is too early to say that eliminating remediation in four-year colleges and universities is a trend; but the interest in this sole-provider status is one to watch. Increased numbers of new first-time students—some predict a more than 75 percent increase over the next decade—will create an enormous demand for services and put a strain on current facilities, staff, and services, especially in light of shrinking financial support from traditional funding sources.

There are growing concerns about other consequences of community colleges' becoming the sole providers of remedial education. Many fear that restricting less well-prepared students to community colleges is breathing new life into higher education's "gatekeeper" mentality: Are four-year colleges and universities reserved only for "college material" students whose test scores indicate that they are college ready? ("Ready or Not" 1995). Current rhetoric suggests that the hierarchical issues are gaining strength—"The promise of American life has always included equal opportunity for all. It has never guaranteed equal results" (Manno 1995, 49).

There is a growing perception that the sole-provider concept will strengthen the notion that community colleges are for less-able students, that one of the community college's roles is to keep students out of universities until they are college ready. Some warn that four-year colleges and universities would take major steps backward in the diversity they have been able to achieve and that the critical integration of remedial work into regular program curriculum would be impossible to achieve.

Will remedial education eventually be eliminated from all community colleges? Why should community colleges in all states be concerned about how New York mayor Rudolph W. Giuliani's plan to eliminate remedial education from the City University of New York community colleges plays out? Because the remediation rates of community colleges in other large urban areas are no better, and many are worse, than the rates in New York. Over the past five years, numbers of state legislators and universities have effectively pushed all responsibility for remedial education onto community colleges; Giuliani's position on remediation—eliminate it from community colleges and privatize it—has been embraced positively by a public that is disaffected with increasingly larger numbers of underprepared students and the higher taxes needed to support them academically.

If other politicians become intrigued with the notion of gaining public support by embracing these ideas, they could carry the banner of eliminating remedial expenditures from colleges across the country. Questions raised by Giuliani's proposal could fuel the push for more privatization of higher education. These questions might include the following: Who would pay for private remedial work? How would assistance be procured? Why would private companies believe that these services would be profitable, and what do they believe about how successful they might be? (Wright 1998).

Many argue that Giuliani's proposal cannot be enforced by law, but he does control the purse strings of the six CUNY community colleges. The perception that we may be witnessing the privatization of American higher education offers community colleges either an opportunity to begin building a strong case for being the primary providers of remedial education, or the chance to step aside from this controversial issue. Some researchers have noted that Giuliani may have done community colleges a service, that remedial education needs to be in the national spotlight so that institutions can have a thorough debate about the effect that doing nothing would have on this large at-risk population and, ultimately, on the way this country conducts its business and itself (McCabe and Day 1998).

Where do we go from here? Remedial education is an educational flash point that will not go away any time soon; nor will the at-risk student. That is not to say that we have ample time to ponder alternatives; we do not. What are we to do with this at-risk population? We now turn to some promising college responses to the belief that remedial education has an important role to play in community colleges.

Chapter 3

At-Risk Students: Getting to Know Johnny

The literature is replete with terms to describe the students who enroll in college academically underprepared for college-level work. The terms *low-achieving, special, disadvantaged, developmental,* and *new,* among others, have a history that reflects different colleges' particular ideologies about who these students are and what approaches should be taken with them. Most of the more common terms are used interchangeably in the literature and in practice, but the terms convey different meanings to the individuals charged with defining them.

Remedial student is a social construct of our own making, one of the unfortunate outcomes of our earliest efforts to tackle the remediation problem. Woven into the history of early remedial efforts is the belief that students who needed remedial work were not as capable as "regular" students, that they did not have the same abilities to learn, and that they might not ever be "college material." Many who taught and administered remedial courses did not, or could not, distinguish between the instruction and the student; the term depicted both a student's capabilities and his or her poor chances for success. To others, it was a convenient label, intended to be no more malevolent than a label given according to a student's discipline: English student, biology student, remedial student.

We prefer the terms *at-risk student* or *underprepared student;* they do less damage and lend themselves to a better focus on the realities of the situation. At best, the term *remedial student* is offensive; at worst it is destructive and insulting. Using this medical metaphor—essentially implying that something is wrong with the student and that some remedy must be applied to effect a cure—is a too-familiar public condemnation. Students neither deserve, nor is there evidence to support, this unfortunate label. However, colleges should not ignore the remediation issue only because the terminology is questionable. Though the students may not need fixing, their academic problems do.

Identifying Students at Risk

The French observe, "You cannot teach French to Johnny until first you *know* Johnny." A number of characteristics put some students at-risk (Roueche and Roueche 1993, 39):

- first-generation learners/little support
- pathways to success unknown
- poor self-image
- have not left neighborhood
- failure/self-defeatism/unreachable goals
- work 30 hours per week/social ills
- average age 28*
- returning women
- large minority student population
- increasing numbers of foreign-born students
- economic insecurity: one-third below poverty level
- desperation/economically driven
- academically weak
- top 99 percent of high school graduating class
- poor or low test scores/GED

This list has changed little in 30 years. The number and variety of students' academic, social, and economic circumstances are overwhelming. Economic realities that predict a bleak future without further education and training drive students to seek that education.

Early on, critics argued that remedial courses were oblique attempts to segregate students by race; enrollment figures documented higher proportions of minority than majority students. The arguments continue, but they are difficult to support. Underprepared students come from all economic situations and geographic areas—although at-risk students are disproportionately minority and poor. These students may be characterized by multiple circumstances, but poverty is their most common denominator. The implicit or explicit linkages between remedial education and race are hard to make when "over 90 percent of *all* colleges

* The average age is now 29.

offer remedial courses to an average of 23 percent of *all students*" (Shaw 1997, 286). Current data indicate that strategies for remedying academic deficiencies are not limited to simple race-based institutional policies.

Looking at the Numbers

Forty percent or more of first-time students entering community colleges are under- or unprepared for college-level courses that require well-developed skills in writing, math, and reading (Smith et al. 1997); consistently over the past 20 years, approximately half of all community college first-time freshmen test as academically deficient and require instruction in at least one subject area (McCabe and Day 1998). However, it is not unusual for community colleges to report that more than 65 percent of their first-time freshmen need basic skill instruction in at least one of the three areas (Milliron and Leach 1998)—most likely in mathematics (NCES 1996). The National Center for Educational Statistics reported in 1996 that approximately 30 percent of all students in higher education take at least one remedial course, freshmen account for more than 50 percent of all students taking basic skills courses, and there is a general pattern of higher remedial enrollments and lower remedial pass rates at public two-year and high-minority enrollment institutions.

Identifying Students Who Need Remedial Work

The National Center for Education Statistics' 1996 report identifies several ways that institutions identify students who need remedial coursework:

- give all entering students placement tests to determine need (the most common method),
- give entering students who meet various criteria (e.g., low SAT/ACT scores* or low GPA) placement tests to determine need,
- require or encourage entering students who meet various criteria to enroll in remedial courses, or
- use some other selection approach (e.g., faculty or staff may refer students for enrollment, or students may refer themselves).

*Other identifiers include the Computerized Placement Test (required by Florida law of all new higher education students; remedial courses are required and must be completed successfully), ASSET, and TASP, the Texas Academic Skills Program test (required by Texas law of all new higher education students; students who fail one or more sections on the test are required to complete remedial instruction successfully before taking upper-level hours or graduating with a degree). A brief survey to test all students' familiarity with academics has been recommended as way to identify those most at risk (Osborne 1997).

Many researchers argue against using standardized tests to determine how well students can perform, or say that standardized tests should not be used alone but rather with other indicators of performance, to get a better picture of the academic deficiencies of at-risk students. For example, criticism about the Texas Academic Skills Program (TASP), a mandatory test for first-time community college students, has called for reducing the pressure for all students to pass. One developmental educator responded: "The legislature will feel that it's accomplished something, the coordinating board will feel that it dodged a political bullet, but lots of unfortunate students will slip through the cracks, and the citizens of Texas will still not have full educational opportunity" (McMillan 1997, A35).

Studying Student Motivation

Studies of students' identification with academics provide both theoretical and empirical evidence that the strength of the tie between academic performance and self-esteem may predict academic success (Osborne 1997). Lower identification with academics has been tied to absenteeism and dropping out, as well as to poor academic performance. Moreover, data from studies of attribution theory of motivation indicate that most at-risk students have positive perceptions of their school experiences or their teachers, but they tend to blame external factors for their poor academic performance—assignments were too difficult, there were too many assignments to complete them all, students were unlucky, students had received inappropriate or poor instruction. These students are characterized as having an external locus of control; that is, they believe that anything and everything in the environment affects what happens to them, and they have little or no control of their experiences. They do not relate their own effort to achievement (Smith and Price 1996). It is possible that by deciding not to invest any of their "selves" in what happens, these students will not identify with academics; furthermore, they will decide not to try. Poor self-esteem is reinforced when students perceive that remedial courses are low-status or dead-end activities and that by enrolling they will be considered less able and less likely to succeed.

There are successful strategies for keeping students enrolled—for example, by keeping students involved with the college through extracurricular, collaborative activities; by building study groups among students in common classes; and by helping students find their own good "fit" with the college (Tinto 1987). At the community college, students are more likely to be enrolled part time, or to drop in and out across a continuum of semesters or quarters; both enrollment characteristics correlate with lower rates of student persistence in studies across all higher education levels (Tinto 1987). The literature describes a variety of successful retention programs that involve students with the institution; while they share many activities, they each reflect the specific interests and available funds at individual colleges. And while the consensus is that these programs are valuable, rarely do the descriptions contain data about the effects of the programs or their outcomes (Dana Center 1998).

Studying Student Performance

We must admit that what we know about the effectiveness of remedial work is too little and too anecdotal; that, too, has changed little in 30 years. However, more recent studies of college transcripts indicate that "there are . . . serious consequences for students taking more than one remedial" course, that "the more [they] take, the less [their] chances of ever getting a bachelor's degree"; moreover, when reading is the core of the problem, "the odds of success in college environments are . . . low" (Adelman 1998, 11). A recent study of remediation in Texas public higher education indicated that more than 95 percent of all students needing remediation will never receive a bachelor's degree (Parker and Ratliff 1998). Reports claim that approximately 50 percent of students enrolled in remedial coursework complete it successfully. Most data reporting students' experiences after leaving remedial courses—that is, how well they fare and what paths they follow—are mixed and flawed. This is an especially disconcerting discovery as these are the data that provide our best tests of the "proof of the pudding."

Studying Student Socialization

At-risk students who are the first in their families to enroll in college have a minimal understanding of the demands that the institution will make or the expectations that it has of its students. The influence of parents and friends, particularly when they are not creating or strengthening interest in college, is tremendous. Presenting orientation courses—preferably ones that last more than a few hours and that cover more than directions to various college units—is a successful way for colleges to intervene. Many colleges require that orientation continue throughout the first semester or quarter of enrollment.

During orientation, students are provided with mentors—teachers and experienced students—who stay in contact with the student and regularly discuss questions and problems. The students are required to participate in collaborative activities, both extracurricular and academic, that strengthen their relationships with peers, and they are required to visit college units that can help with such services as applying for financial aid and finding affordable childcare facilities. Some colleges report that better student evaluations and improved GPAs are two outcomes of enrolling students in cohort groups (groups that take all classes together for the first semester or quarter, follow a "study buddy" system, and participate in extracurricular activities that require spending time together in pursuit of an assignment or social event) and that these outcomes have made the time and complexity of the effort required during the registration process worthwhile.

Conclusion

The at-risk student is a complex being who requires community colleges to bring every creative talent to solutions that are "just plain difficult and sometimes just not known" (McClenney 1998, 2).

> How do you provide effective remedial education to a single mother with three children, a 40-hour per week job, and no transportation, who reads at the 6th grade level (perhaps with limited English proficiency), who has had a lousy experience with school and suffers from incredibly low self-esteem, and who wants desperately to create a better life for herself and her family? And, how do you help this person advance about eight grade levels in a few months (with no more second chances), use technology only when technology works best, provide human support when only "high touch" will do, and ultimately provide documented, quantified (but reader-friendly) evidence of success that only the devil himself could deny? How, exactly? (McClenney 1998, 2–3)

Chapter 4

Remedial Courses and Programs: Looking at the How's

The key to making remedial education work is achieving a fit between will and action, between documented success and the unique culture of a college. Individual colleges may custom design and implement special strategies by judging the merits and particulars of others' goals and measuring the results of others' strategies against their own, thereby establishing or augmenting existing programs.

This chapter provides current data to answer many of the common questions about remedial education issues; summarizes the most useful information gleaned from a brief survey of selected community colleges that was conducted during the writing of this report; and addresses how several colleges have succeeded with at-risk students.

Some Common Questions about Remediation in Higher Education

What types of credit are assigned to remedial work? Eighty percent of public two-year colleges award institutional credit—that is, credit that applies toward financial aid or full-time student status but not toward degree completion—for remedial reading, writing, and mathematics courses (NCES 1996). Other types of credit for remedial work include degree credit that counts toward subject requirements and degree credit that counts toward elective requirements. It is rare for a college to offer no credit for remedial courses.

Do colleges require remedial work of students whose assessment test results indicate academic deficiencies? Voluntary compliance continues to be a weak link in remedial programs nationwide. Leaving the decision to enroll in remedial courses in the hands of underprepared students, especially where assessment tests indicate significantly low levels of skill development, is unjustified. Some argue that community college students are adults who should be allowed to make these decisions for themselves. However, because other programs and courses justify and enforce their prerequisites, the voluntary nature of enrolling in remediation is a curious phenomenon. According to the National Center for Education Statistics (1996), about 75 percent of all reporting institutions indicated that remedial courses were mandatory; however, students in public two-year colleges were required to enroll in remedial coursework less often than those in public or private four-year institutions.

How do colleges identify students who need remedial work? Colleges use placement tests to identify at-risk students. Research indicates that test scores should be used in conjunction with other predictors to get a more valid picture of student deficiencies. For more than two decades, people have argued that if achievement tests are used to place students in remedial courses, alternate tests should be used after remedial work has been completed to test students' readiness for regular college work.

Do colleges allow students who are enrolled in remedial work to take regular academic courses? Most colleges allow students to enroll in regular courses after they have remediated the skills that the regular courses require. For students who are enrolled in remedial reading courses, the choices in regular coursework are limited. However, students who must complete only a remedial course in mathematics can choose from a larger selection of regular courses. Nationwide, policies on students taking regular academic courses while they take remedial courses vary: Some institutions place no restrictions on the regular academic courses that students can take while they are taking remedial courses; others do not allow students to take any regular academic courses while enrolled in remedial courses; still others allow students enrolled in remedial courses to take regular courses that do not require the skills the students are currently developing in remedial courses (NCES 1996).

Where are remedial courses housed in the college? The majority of institutions that offer remedial reading, writing, and mathematics teach those courses in their traditional academic departments. Fewer institutions have separate divisions for remedial instruction. It is not uncommon for separate remedial divisions to control entry-level remedial courses and to share the responsibility for second-level remedial courses with individual academic departments. Some of the stronger remedial programs are housed in departments responsible for all student services and support initiatives. Fewer than 12 percent of all institutions nationwide use learning centers; more public two-year colleges than private offer remedial writing and mathematics courses in separate divisions, and institutions with high minority enrollment provide remedial instruction through separate divisions more often than do institutions with low minority enrollment (NCES 1996).

Whether students should be grouped homogeneously or heterogeneously, a question that dates back almost 75 years, continues to be contentious; little progress has been made toward resolving the argument. The wider the range of skills and abilities among students in a classroom, the greater the instructional problems for any teacher.

Where are classes in English as a second language (ESL) housed in the college? ESL courses are housed in adult basic education departments as frequently as in remedial programs. A few colleges that enroll a large number of new immigrants or that operate in communities with high numbers of foreign-born and second-generation families house ESL courses in a separate department. Nationwide, about half of all institutions that enroll freshmen students offer ESL courses (NCES 1996). As many institutions as not consider ESL courses to be remedial. Institutions whose minority enrollment is high indicate that their ESL courses are remedial more often than do their counterparts with lower minority enrollment.

Do states have policies or laws governing colleges' remedial efforts? As more legislators question offering remedial courses in their states' four-year colleges and universities, pressure to justify where and by whom remedial education will be offered will intensify. Currently, one-third of all institutions that offer remedial courses report that state policies or laws affect the remedial education they offer, usually by requiring or encouraging them to offer remedial education. More public four-year than public two-year institutions are discouraged from offering remedial education, or their offerings are restricted (NCES 1996).

How much time do students have to complete their remedial work? Within the last five years, more colleges have reported increased outside pressure to limit the number of semesters or quarters that students may enroll in remedial coursework, or to limit the number of times a student may enroll in any one skills course. A few states limit the time a student may spend in remedial work or the number of attempts a student may make to complete the work successfully. Recent meetings of college trustees have included open debates about limiting the number, and discussion of such options as "college-ready" certificates that would be earned by students completing instruction at self-contained institutes on campus (Locksley 1998). Nationwide, only about one-fourth of all institutions limit the length of time a student may take remedial courses; of those, 75 percent report that those limits were set by institutional policy and 21 percent report they were set by state policy or law (NCES 1996).

Who teaches remedial courses? The majority of colleges indicate that their remedial courses are taught by both full- and part-time faculty, but far more often by part-time faculty. National survey data suggest that far more part-time than full-time faculty are hired to teach remedial and developmental courses than to teach any other programs or courses (Roueche, Roueche, and Milliron 1995). Some researchers observe that colleges may use large percentages of part-time faculty to teach at-risk students because few full-time faculty want to work with them and prefer to "avoid having much contact with them by hiring part-time instructors from the outside to do the work" (Astin 1998, 12).

Although there is strong evidence that part-time faculty perform as well as or better than full-time faculty, in most disciplines or technical areas, using a large percentage of part-time faculty to teach remedial education will be problematic unless a college's high expectations for remedial education are reflected in its hiring practices. Instructors who thoroughly understand a college's goals and the complexity of the at-risk population, who have significant classroom experience and a broad repertoire of teaching techniques that lets them match learning needs to instruction, who want to work collaboratively with other faculty, who want to be involved in strong faculty development activities, who *want to teach remedial courses,* and who *believe that at-risk students can learn* and be successful—these are the right instructors for the job, whether they are full time or part time. Faculty attitude and competence are the keys to student success.

How are remedial programs evaluated? Program evaluation has been and remains the weakest component of the remedial effort. Most colleges have never defined, described, or evaluated their remediation efforts very well. The 30-year-old question remains: Can student academic deficiencies be remedied? Some programs have shown that they can, absolutely. These programs have succeeded by setting high standards against which to evaluate their efforts; asking tough questions about program design, teaching methods, and outcomes; and establishing mechanisms by which to make changes when outcomes or results do not meet expectations or achieve agreed-upon levels of success. For example, they ask:

- What are acceptable levels of student success in the various skill areas? What percentage of students should be successful in one attempt at course completion? In two? Should there, or can there, be more time allotted for completion?
- What is an acceptable level of student success in regular courses following the remedial instruction?

We still do not know very much about the actual success of remedial programs because colleges do not evaluate them very well. They frequently collect inappropriate or poor-quality data and use inappropriate criteria for measuring effectiveness. Community colleges must invest more time and look with a more critical eye at how they evaluate their remedial programs—both to challenge the public myths about their effectiveness and to improve program performance.

How effective are remedial programs? Effectiveness criteria and data are mixed, at best; most data are anecdotal. Colleges' collection policies and data types are fragmented and uneven. However, data from some effectiveness studies are encouraging and provide a good place to begin discussions about what should be measured. For example, a majority of students who complete remedial courses do as well or better in regular courses than do students who did not require remedial work (Boylan and Bonham 1992; NCES 1995), and one-third of Florida community college graduates transferring to universities had completed developmental programs (McCabe 1995). The major sticking point is this: The majority of community colleges do not know how effective their remediation is because they do not assess their effectiveness very well, do not know how to assess it, or do not want to know.

How much do remedial courses and programs cost? The issue of effectiveness is followed closely by the issue of cost. Unfortunately, there is a paucity of college data about the cost of remedial education. Of course, there are still those who believe that the cost—any cost—is too high, that the money should be used for students who have a better chance of being successful, or that any remediation is an unnecessary or unjustified expense in higher education.

Cost data reflect major differences in the total numbers of new and returning students, whether the remedial program or course is mandatory or voluntary, regardless of the particular activities that a college designates as remedial, and despite other unique college or statewide characteristics. Costs range from Wyoming's $7.5 million in academic year 1995–96 (with disclaimers that colleges keep enrollments in developmental courses smaller than in regular courses to provide more tutorial assistance to at-risk students), to Florida's $50 million, to Texas's $155 million in 1996–97 (an increase of 279 percent in eight years in spending for remediation, compared with an increase of 49 percent in other higher education appropriations). Among a number of colleges with strong remedial programs, costs range from 2.7 percent of the total college budget to 27.3 percent, with an average of approximately 8 percent.

Some researchers argue that remedial work is not as costly as the public has come to believe. Many public officials believe that the percentage of students enrolling in remedial work in community colleges is the same as the percentage of the college budget spent on remediation; data simply do not support that belief (McCabe and Day 1998). Rather, only a third of students who need remedial work need courses in all three areas; most need to take one remedial course and complete that course in their first semester; and students, on average, take only about five remedial credits (McCabe 1995; Blanchette 1997). McCabe and Day (1998, 30) also reveal the following:

- The cost to the state and other local funding sources for remedial education is only about 16 to 23 percent of the annual costs for supporting a full-time student.
- In most states the annual public cost to remediate a community college student is less than $1,000—a far cry from what is assumed by most critics.
- A 1997 Department of Education study found that only 8 percent of federal financial aid to community college students is used for remedial courses.
- When community college and university data are combined, the percentage of federal financial aid funds used to support remedial courses totals only 4 percent.

The costs of remediation in college should be kept in perspective. As Derek Bok observed, "If you think the cost of education is high—try ignorance" (1979, 28). The cost of remedial education that works is small compared with the cost of maintaining a society with high numbers of uneducated, unemployed, unemployable, and discontented citizens. Remedial programs have the potential to alleviate these costly social ills and offer opportunities for citizens to become taxpayers, workers, and, ultimately, consumers.

Do private, for-profit partnerships with entities outside the college help improve delivery and student success rates in remedial courses and programs? Joint ventures between community colleges and private companies to provide remedial services are in their infancy. Some of these ventures have been successful, but others have been disappointing and ineffective. What is clear thus far is that there must be strong collaboration between a college and a private, for-profit entity that attempts such a venture.

Some Common Characteristics of Successful Remedial Programs in Community Colleges

Many community colleges have defined clear goals, mounted initiatives, and implemented policies that hold great promise for all colleges struggling to establish successful remedial education courses and programs. Most of what we know is that a total program approach to the complex needs of at-risk students—a systemic approach—has the greatest potential for success. Moreover, the program should be but one part of an institutionwide commitment to success for all students that includes student development professionals collaborating with faculty and staff to implement policies that will improve student retention, achievement, and graduation rates. We begin this discussion of successful components with the following recommendations drawn from our 1993 study of remedial programs, *Between a Rock and a Hard Place*. These recommendations incorporate the majority of findings from major studies of program success conducted over the last decade.

Colleges must increase the support and structure they offer at-risk students, who need support and structure more than any other students in higher education. Unfortunately, many community college leaders and faculty are hesitant to implement academic standards that would improve student persistence and achievement, clinging to the notion that the "open door" means access and that structure limits access. Nothing could be further from the truth: Students should not be able to sample from the entire curriculum, and enrollment will not go down if colleges require too much of incoming students. Rather, there are strong data to indicate that implementing rigorous academic policies and procedures improves student success and increases college enrollments.

Expand pre-enrollment activities. Include students in junior high and high school in pre-enrollment activities. Any potential student who contacts the college should receive a prompt note or a call to follow up, as well as an application and financial aid form. The key is to personalize the college for the potential student.

Require orientation. Orientation is provided far better in four-year colleges and universities than in community colleges. Community colleges could help orient new students by matching them with mentors, perhaps second-year students with similar major interests or courses.

Abolish late registration. Everyone is ill served by someone who comes late to a class that is established and underway. The first days of a course are important for setting the tone for the semester or quarter, and for clarifying expectations for performance. If late registration is institutional policy, then the last day of late registration should be the day before classes begin. This recommendation would not apply to programs designed as self-paced or for daily entry.

Make assessment and placement mandatory. Colleges can be too willing to believe that they have made a mistake, that assessment tests did not measure basic skill development accurately. While the results may not be accurate without a doubt, the more common test results are valid indicators that students have a problem (although tests rarely provide clear indications of specific problems). Universities do not hesitate to prohibit students from enrolling in courses for which they are not prepared or have not completed prerequisites; community colleges should do no less.

Eliminate simultaneous enrollment in skill and regular academic courses that require the skill for which remediation is advised or mandated. Although common practice, enrolling in skill and regular academic courses simultaneously should be eliminated or carefully monitored. For example, for a student whose reading levels are low and who has not completed the remedial reading course successfully, enrolling in a course with heavy reading assignments is ill advised. Some colleges argue that students are more motivated when they are allowed to take courses in their interest area or major. But the inability to handle the workload or to meet the skill demands of such courses will not motivate students to continue.

Require working students to take fewer hours. Colleges should require working students to take fewer hours in proportion to the number of hours they work each week. For example, a student who works 30 hours a week should be limited to six academic hours; one who works 20 hours a week, to nine academic hours. Because more and more students are working longer hours, a five- or six-year degree plan is not uncommon at universities, and the "two-year" degree is now more likely to take three or four years to complete.

Provide more comprehensive financial aid programs. There are strong data to indicate that students who receive financial aid have higher retention rates than those who do not seek it or want it, and receiving financial aid helps ease students' concerns about encumbering themselves or their families with more debt (Astin 1985; Jackson 1988). Students should receive information about financial aid sources and opportunities early on; work-study programs should be tied to course and other workload arrangements; and information about available part-time work, budget counseling, and emergency loan services should be available.

Establish peer and faculty mentors and support groups. Even with work and family responsibilities, at-risk students need to have ties to the college, to feel connected to the institution, and to enjoy relationships with others who care about what happens to them and who can provide important information and support about academic and personal experiences. Courses and programs that build mentoring and support groups into their designs help accommodate students' schedules.

Require literacy activities in all courses in all discipline areas. Basic skills should be developed in remedial courses and practiced in regular college work. Someone in the college should be responsible for asking instructors what reading and writing activities are required in their courses and for inspecting examples of student work that meet instructors' requirements.

Increase the impact of classroom instruction by providing time for skill practice and development with supplemental instruction and tutoring. Tutoring, study groups, learning assistance centers, and other academic support services expand opportunities for learning that are limited by scheduled class periods and teacher-student ratios.

Recruit, develop, and hire the best faculty. Whether full- or part-time faculty are employed to teach at-risk students, they should be eager to teach them, flexible in their teaching strategies to accommodate students' needs, and willing to spend the additional time and energy that at-risk students require.

Evaluate student and program outcomes regularly and disseminate the findings. Evaluations should include definitions of what colleges want to achieve, clear descriptions about viable outcomes, and mechanisms for evaluating whether outcomes have been achieved.

Colleges must become more humane organizations. In tinkering with the system, a community college can flex its most creative muscles. Identifying individual groups of students and addressing their needs are the strengths of many exemplary programs; however, the entire college must be committed to serving all students.

We add a final, critical recommendation to the previous list, drawn from more recent data about successful remedial program designs:

Remedial programs should be flexible. Successful programs document good results from such "thinking out of the box" experiments as eliminating lock-step scheduling of remedial courses and moving away from the more traditional time frames. For example, intensive short-term sessions prior to skills testing increase test scores or accelerate student performance in follow-on remedial coursework, and open-entry, open-exit skills courses accommodate student diversity in skill-deficiency levels. Students respond to the opportunity to choose from multiple approaches to remediation. It is difficult to motivate students to work through a long, protracted schedule of courses, even when they have been convinced that they need the instruction. Students who are allowed to enroll in regular coursework while completing remedial work are more motivated to continue—but only if the regular coursework does not demand that the student have a high level of the same skills that have not yet been developed through remedial work.

Recent Lessons from Selected Community Colleges

Survey responses and program descriptions from more than 50 community colleges, punctuated by some conversations with program principals, provided interesting updates to the information given thus far in this chapter:

- Assessment tests for first-time students are mandatory in every college surveyed.
- Even without state-mandated policies, the majority of colleges are inclined to require that students enroll in remedial courses in areas in which tests identify them as being weak, and require that remedial work be completed before students enroll in regular coursework, including occupational programs.
- Remedial programs and courses are provided by separate departments as often as they are offered within established academic departments. Some colleges offer entrance-level developmental work within an intensive support program; follow-on remedial courses are taught within individual academic departments with support from the established intensive program.
- English-as-a-second-language programs are as often housed in developmental departments as in adult basic education or English departments. Some colleges do not assess tuition and fees for ESL courses.
- Colleges report wide variations in what they charge to students for remedial education—from regular tuition to graduated increases for repeated efforts—and in the time they allow students to complete remedial work, ranging from beginning the remedial sequence in the first semester and taking one remedial course per semester until all required courses have been completed, to no time limits.
- The majority of colleges do not allow students enrolled in remedial work to enroll in college-level courses, courses that count toward degree completion, or courses that carry college credit.
- More than 80 percent of first-time students tested as deficient in one or more basic skills and were enrolled in remedial work.
- Completion or success rates ranged from 34 to 93 percent of all students attempting remedial work.

- Fewer than 2 percent of the responding colleges currently employ or partner with outside providers specifically for remedial services.
- All colleges report that a combination of full-time and part-time faculty—but more part-time—teach remedial courses.
- Most colleges use some instructional technology in their remedial courses, primarily computers for writing assignments and mathematical problem solving.

Improved institutionwide support for increased student services was a common thread among the responses. Such support took many forms, including

- development of learning communities within the program and collegewide
- enhanced faculty, tutor, and staff development activities focused on student services
- increased use of college support services by all students
- increased college focus on proper placement in remedial and regular courses
- development of comprehensive programs, including a "success" orientation for all degree-seeking students
- implementation of a case management process for most at-risk students
- increased use of department tests to determine student success levels and percentages
- making completion of the remedial sequence an institutional priority

The survey also requested descriptions of any major successes, such as orientation or cohort activities, that have helped make remediation efforts a success. Among the responses were these descriptions:

Metropolitan Community College, Nebraska: After pilot testing a learning community for high-risk development students for approximately one year, reports are that retention and student success rates have increased significantly. Although too soon to make an accurate assessment of long-term impact, well over 80 percent of the students are completing their courses and being retained into succeeding quarters. In addition, the development of interdisciplinary curriculum and the opportunity for faculty to develop professionally have been positive unanticipated outcomes of the experiment.

Valencia Community College, Florida: The most effective programmatic boost to the college preparatory program is to enroll the student in the Student Success course simultaneously with college preparatory courses (VCC's remedial/developmental sequence). Studies have indicated that students simultaneously enrolled in the second-level English and reading (9th- through 12th-grade-level work) *and* certain college-level courses do almost as well as students not mandated into college preparatory courses at all. Similarly, performance of students who have completed their required college preparatory courses do nearly as well as students who placed into all college-level courses upon first enrollment. Another boost is the development of new faculty training programs to infuse active learning into college preparatory courses through a Title III project and the current Underprepared Student Initiative. Results from pilot sections of college preparatory courses have shown dramatic increases in student success rates, some increasing by as much as 75 percent. The college is still in a developmental mode in these efforts, but early data promise significant improvement.

Schoolcraft College, Michigan: In the Peer Assisted Learning (PAL) program, faculty identify students who completed their courses successfully. The student is paid to retake the class and serve as a faculty assistant, and assist with facilitating study groups. The program coordinator collects attendance and grades to evaluate program effectiveness. In Writing Fellows, faculty identify students who are excellent writers. These students are hired to serve as peer reviewers in courses requesting a Writing Fellow. The program, modeled after the Writing Fellows program at Brown University, has been extremely successful. In Paired Reading Courses (learning communities), reading and study skills courses are linked to content courses. Students learn how to read specific textbooks and how to take lecture notes in the linked courses. Faculty in both courses work closely together to ensure effectiveness. The content of the linked course is used heavily in the reading/study skills course.

Two Success Stories: The Community College of Denver and Greenville Technical College

Two colleges that help illustrate successful approaches to the remediation problem are the Community College of Denver (CCD), for a decade's commitment to success for all students and special attention to increasing success rates among students of color, and Greenville Technical College (GTC), South Carolina, for its experimental partnership linking college faculty and staff with an outside provider of remedial services.

The Community College of Denver is the most diverse of all Colorado higher-education institutions in terms of race and ethnicity of students and staff. One vision statement, written at the conclusion of the 1996 academic year, proposed that "success rates of students of all races, classes, and cultures will be comparably high." Attending to recruitment, retention, graduation, and celebration to support diversity has had dramatic results; in 1997, CCD reported that credit enrollment of minority students had increased from 27 percent to 54 percent in a decade. Among the successful outcomes that have been achieved are these extraordinary examples: (1) minority students have increased from 13 percent to 42.5 percent of the total number of students graduating or transferring to a four-year college, and students of color are as likely as white students to finish their courses of study or graduate (Roueche and Roueche 1998); and (2) degree-seeking students who begin their work in remedial courses are as likely to complete their first semester successfully, continue their college studies, and graduate or transfer as other degree-seeking students (McClenney and Flores 1998).

CCD has been committed to student learning for a decade. All courses are competency-based. Developmental courses and support services are evaluated by staff within each unit of the Division of Education and Academic Services, one of CCD's six instructional departments and home to the developmental program. All data used to assess program performance are shared with faculty, students, and leaders in the community.

Following are some of the indicators of success identified and monitored by CCD as well as some points about what CCD has learned:

- 84.5 percent of students in the Division of Education and Academic Services had a GPA of 2.00 or higher during the 1995–96 academic year.

- In student evaluations of faculty for the 1995–96 academic year, faculty in the Division of Education and Academic Services rated slightly higher than college faculty overall.
- 88 percent of students in reading classes received a grade of C or higher during the 1995–96 academic year.
- 92 percent of students who used the reading lab three hours or more per week had a GPA of 2.00 or higher during the spring 1996 semester.
- 97 percent of students who used the writing lab three hours or more per week had a GPA of 2.00 or higher during the spring 1996 semester.
- 81 percent of English-as-a-second-language students received a grade of C or higher during the fall 1995 semester.
- 91 percent of Special Learning Support Program students received an overall GPA of 2.00 or higher during the 1995–96 academic year.
- 93 percent of Student Support Services students had a GPA of 2.00 or higher during the 1995–96 academic year.
- 82 percent of Supplemental Services students had a GPA of 2.00 or higher during summer and fall 1996. (McClenney and Flores 1998, 50–51)

CCD keeps its institutional eye on "what is possible" with vision statements about desirable outcomes and related plans. Its model focuses on and keeps the college moving toward what is possible

In February 1997, **Greenville Technical College** entered into a partnership with Kaplan Learning Services and established these partnership goals:

- Provide a more "user-friendly" assessment experience for prospective students.
- Improve the image of developmental studies by adding relevant content and faster results in helping students progress into their program of choice, including fast-track or flexible entry points to accept students and exit them at different points in the term.
- Improve enrollment through better retention. (Grastie 1998a, 60)

GTC worked with Kaplan to implement test review workshops to familiarize students with the COMPASS and ASSET entry assessment tests. A six-hour workshop, College Success Skills, provides instruction of two hours each in reading, writing, and mathematics for students who have either failed their first attempt at the test or who are anxious about how well they will perform on their first effort. Students who have taken the test and done poorly can retest after the workshop. The sessions are taught on campus by GTC employees and have alleviated many students' anxieties about the assessment process, about potential developmental work, and about going to college.

In August 1997, GTC implemented new courses in reading, writing, and mathematics after a Kaplan-facilitated process to "re-invent" GTC's developmental courses "so that they would look, feel, and be like a college-level course and tie directly to future courses, texts, and careers" (Grastie 1998a, 62). The new courses are GTC courses taught by GTC faculty to GTC students. The Kaplan partnership does not threaten faculty security; rather, it aims to create a more cost-effective system of instruction. It works to improve all facets of the students' relationships with the college; to connect students with follow-on courses to their remedial work; and to involve faculty in maintaining course standards and integrity, while allowing them to bring their own personalities to their classes.

In spring 1998 correspondence (Grastie 1998b), GTC documented that students in the Kaplan-partnered courses achieved results as good as or better than those achieved by students in non-Kaplan courses. Highlights include:

- Reading: In the lower-level course, more non-Kaplan students (45 percent) than Kaplan students (36 percent) earned passing grades, but a higher portion of Kaplan students (34 percent) than non-Kaplan students (32 percent) earned grades of A.
- English: While similar percentages of Kaplan students (45 percent) and non-Kaplan students (44 percent) earned passing grades in the lower-level course and more non-Kaplan students (63 percent) than Kaplan students (50 percent) earned passing grades in the higher-level course, far more Kaplan students (28 percent) earned grades of A than did non-Kaplan students (0 percent).
- Math: In the lower-level course, more Kaplan students (58 percent) than non-Kaplan students (53 percent) earned passing grades. In the higher-level course, similar percentages of Kaplan students (46 per-

cent) and non-Kaplan students (45 percent) earned passing grades. According to follow-up data for students who were in the Kaplan courses during fall semester, a greater portion of Kaplan students than non-Kaplan students earned passing grades in follow-on math courses.

- In spring 1998, there was a 6 percent higher re-enrollment rate among students who had taken Kaplan courses in fall 1997 than among students who had not taken Kaplan courses that fall.
- For COMPASS Workshop Review participants, the data have been extended to determine enrollment for those students who took the workshop from April 1, 1997, to March 31, 1998. These figures indicate that more than 90 percent of the workshop students enrolled either fall 1997 or spring 1998, as opposed to 75 percent of those who did not take the workshop.

During spring 1998, the departments asked the administration to consider having all courses and all faculty involved in the Kaplan partnership. As a result of faculty input, beginning in fall 1998, all classes in basic and advanced reading, writing, and mathematics in the developmental studies area implemented the Kaplan-partnered course materials and teaching strategies. Sixty full-time and part-time faculty participated in professional development activities by Kaplan staff during the summer and worked with the Kaplan curriculum development team to prepare for the conversion of the curriculum. All advanced math courses are using a new text that was developed in a collaborative effort between GTC math faculty and Kaplan Learning Services. The texts for the basic math course and the language arts courses are under development using faculty input and guidance.

GTC further reports that important benefits have been achieved by involving all faculty in the program. The continuity from course to course, and from classroom to classroom, is critical to producing results overall. Faculty are part of a team in which all instructors are using the same text, and there is constant dialogue among instructors and Kaplan staff to make refinements, suggestions, and continuous improvements as teachers interact with students in the classroom and use the new materials. Professional development has focused on the text, software, group and writing activities, and grading. In math, all faculty are using equivalent chapter tests as well as final exams, so there is a better opportunity to measure the readiness of all students for their next math course. In the language arts courses, faculty are implementing software and word processing with students as they incorporate college-level transferable skills in these classes. Feedback from both faculty and students is positive, especially about the high level of student-generated active learning in the language arts classes and the new text in the advanced math course.

Colleges collaborating with outside providers is a young idea that has not yet proved to be in the best interests of the institution and its students. Greenville Technical College admits that the effort has been both exasperating and exhilarating for the developmental team, but claims that these efforts have heightened the entire institution's appreciation for the work of the developmental staff and the importance of the developmental program to the college. Trends in student performance after enrolling in regular courses will be the proof of the pudding and will provide informed direction for text and course revisions.

Conclusion

We like Pogrow's definition: "An exemplary program is one that can increase learning to a surprising extent with a great deal of consistency" (1998, 22). For programs to be successful, they must reflect the unique characteristics and cultures of their colleges. They must blend the common and the unique in order to achieve a standard of excellence with which an institution and its community can live.

It is by asking and answering the most difficult questions that a college can best evaluate its remedial programs. Perhaps colleges should begin any evaluation by crafting the questions that challenge them the most, and which they hope others will not ask them before they have time to draft an adequate response. Or perhaps all colleges should begin by answering the tough, more public questions that other colleges are being required to answer now. How colleges behave now in response to their communities' intense interest in student success will determine the quality of their existence in the next decades.

Chapter 5

Recommendations and Conclusions

"Providing effective 'remedial' education would do more to alleviate our most serious social and economic problems than almost any other action we could take."
—Alexander W. Astin (1998, 12)

If the year 2000 becomes "a psychological watershed" as predicted (Comer 1996, 8), nowhere is it more likely to do so than in community colleges. Over the past 30 years, we have researched some of the most serious challenges to community colleges. Not one of the challenges has remained so controversial, has so divided community colleges ideologically, and has remained so resistant to change as has remedial education.

It is a tragedy that there has been so little progress toward establishing better systems of remedial education. It is mind-boggling that educational institutions have not joined together to prevent the serious threat that a large population of at-risk students presents to America's economic and social well-being. Even the appearance of broad-based resolve or strategy continues to be just out of reach of the academy, and the responses of individual colleges to the problems of remedial education remain loosely defined as to purpose and largely unexamined as to outcome.

It is not surprising that a heightened interest in the possibilities of success and the consequences of failure with at-risk students is driving unprecedented investigation into the way colleges embrace remedial education; it is surprising that it has taken so long to occur. It is clear that if community colleges do not better address remedial education, this country will suffer enormous consequences.

This survey compiles current thinking and events, but we do not attempt closure here. Rather, we attempt a beginning by sharing our observations in order to inform and encourage, and by drawing from them some recommendations for future action. This is the bird's-eye view:

> Students are leaving high school no better prepared than they were in the mid-1960s. In fact, evidence indicates that despite higher grade point averages, these students'

> skills and competencies are at the lowest levels in American history. Moreover, we are not talking only about literacy, or unprepared or underprepared students as viewed from their mastery or their attainment of cognitive skills; we are looking at a new generation of adult learners characterized by economic, social, personal, and academic insecurities. They are older adults, with family and other financial responsibilities that require part-time, or often full-time, jobs in addition to coursework requirements; they are first-generation learners with unclear notions of their college roles and their goals; they are members of minority and foreign-born groups; they have poor self-images and doubt their abilities to be successful; and they have limited world experiences that further narrow the perspectives they can bring to options in their lives." (Roueche and Roueche 1993, 246)

Serving as a backdrop for these realities is the community colleges' "mission blur," which was created in part by the challenge of being all things to all people; of facing classroom climates that are negatively affected by inner-city decline and poverty and by single-parent adults with little time to improve their lives; of grappling with the public misconception that there are too few jobs rather than too few people trained to do them; and of gearing up for the public school dropouts who condemn future generations of children to poverty and undereducation and America to higher crime and lower productivity. Unfortunately, "these issues may only appear to be traveling parallel paths . . . [but] they will collide . . . on many fronts with such magnitude that viable repair cannot occur for decades" (Roueche and Roueche 1993, 247). Since we wrote those words, our future has become our present.

Recommendations

Overarching recommendation: Survey the landscape for proactive responses. The remedial education landscape includes some extraordinarily successful structures; that is good news. Some community colleges have tackled the problems of academic unpreparedness for at least a decade and have documented their success thoroughly. They have made the tough decisions and committed themselves to seeing them through before outside forces compelled them to do so. They had a clear vision of the need to identify goals—a vision that at the time must have appeared lofty, but that put them on a path to good progress—and to evaluate their progress critically and judiciously. The community colleges are the first to acknowledge that the tasks of agreement and implementation were not easy, but that the rewards are worth the effort. The successes they have achieved with academically at-risk students may be as exciting for these colleges as discovering that they are in far better positions to respond to current questions and criticisms of community colleges' performance with all students.

By stepping up to the task of responding to the challenges that at-risk populations bring and achieving some success, these colleges have married goals that critics argue are mutually exclusive—the goals of access and excellence. Kay McClenney, vice president of the Education Commission of the States, argues that the will to achieve any transformation, or change, is critical to success:

> For more than a decade I have been watching the transformational process in one particular community college—at the Community College of Denver. I have watched while, with tight resources, CCD's people have doubled enrollment, while also dramatically increasing student diversity and student outcomes, defining methods of assessing and documenting student learning, and most incredibly, virtually eliminating the achievement gap between minority and nonminority students. It did take ten years of work. But the first thing it took was deciding to do it. (McClenney 1998, 4)

Some might be surprised that efforts to succeed with at-risk students could so dramatically change the entire institution, that everyone stands to profit by efforts to meet the needs of those most in need of instruction and support. We contend that, considering what we know today about improving students' academic performance, this outcome should not be surprising at all.

There is so much more to learn about what and how success has been achieved with at-risk students. The programs described in this document provide some flavor of the excellent places at which to begin a search. From this "good news" observation, we make these recommendations to community colleges:

Recommendation 1: Examine the essential characteristics and components of other institutions' successful remedial courses and programs, not necessarily in the interest of adopting their strategies, but perhaps of adapting them. No plans are as appealing to implement or as successful as those that carry the "made here" stamp; however, there are no reasons good enough and no time to reinvent the wheel.

Recommendation 2: Employ a more collaborative effort to learn from each other. There is no reason to hang, separately or together. Over the past few years, researchers have identified colleges with successful remedial programs or program components. We believe that there are other successes that will remain unknown because college leaders and remediation professionals either do not disseminate information or do not disseminate it widely and effectively.

Recommendation 3: Ask the questions about your own performance that are being asked about others, and take action. For example, an institution might study the core performance indicators in South Carolina and Colorado; their history of study, development, implementation, and revision makes them excellent documents with which to begin developing criteria for measuring program effectiveness. Colleges should collect data about goal achievement; most colleges do not understand, or fail to make, the critical links between goal and expected outcomes in identifying the appropriate data to be collected. Every community college should consider how well its program measures up against the criteria other colleges use to measure and report their performance. No college should ignore questions that policymakers, media, and community members ask about its performance, whether national or local. Flash points know no physical boundaries, and news travels fast.

The federal Government Performance and Results Act (GPRA), now in the hands of community colleges, provides guidelines for all federal funding proposals submitted March 2000 and beyond. In a 1998 booklet titled "Demonstrating Results," the Office of Higher Education Programs (HEP) identifies the GPRA guidelines as a long-term process "to change . . . focus from activities generated and resources expended to *results achieved* [italics added]" (iii). The booklet's foreword continues:

> To do this effectively, we must develop plans to operate more efficiently to achieve our missions, set performance

> goals for ourselves and our programs, measure how well these goals are achieved, and make the results available to Congress and to our constituents. This is significantly different from the operational focus of the past which measured success merely by the number of grants awarded and the numbers of students served. To demonstrate and document program effectiveness clearly, we must collaborate throughout the grant cycle on critical activities that are designed to achieve and document the goals for which our programs were established and funded. (iii)

This language has the familiar sound of institutional effectiveness mandates. Colleges will change how they describe their performance or risk losing federal funding. Funding for subsequent years will be reviewed annually; even the Department of Education's anticipated increases in funding each year will be subject to review and must demonstrate program effectiveness. A number of statements from this booklet will drive a virtual whirlwind of changes in the language and intent of funding proposals:

- Even if a program is desirable, appropriations will be forthcoming only to the extent that positive outcomes can be demonstrated.
- The Government Performance and Results Act is the tool Congress has established to obtain objective information about program performance that will assist it in making the hard choices on what will be funded and what will not.
- Effort was often substituted for results. This is no longer acceptable.
- GPRA *is the law.*
- The annual performance plan provides the accountability that is the centerpiece of GPRA.
- In some cases, the data that are needed are not now being collected and, in others, the validity and comparability of the data are poor.
- While site visits traditionally have been conducted to assure compliance with statutes and program regulations, the emphasis in the future will be on performance in line with the project and program objectives. ("Demonstrating Results" 1998, 3–17)

The booklet stresses the importance of collaboration and demonstration, and concludes: "It is part of an effort to determine what we will do, how we will do it, and what we will accomplish" (24), a directive that is strikingly similar to one written 30 years ago: "The junior colleges must now determine what students are going to learn in remedial programs, the conditions of learning, and how this learning can be evaluated" (Roueche 1968, 50).

Recommendation 4: Provide a holistic approach to programs for at-risk students. If colleges are totally committed to being successful with at-risk students, they must be prepared to think holistically. At-risk students come to college with such diverse needs that stand-alone services or classes—no matter how successful in helping at-risk students—will not achieve a college's larger goal of retaining these students and helping them achieve their own goals of improved performance and academic success. A successful learning lab, a strong reading program, or an excellent mathematics program, if offered as a stand-alone instructional service or class, falls far short of the broader institutional commitment that colleges must make.

At-risk students have dramatic needs for financial aid, help with childcare and transportation, and other assistance. It takes collaborative effort from multiple entities to achieve a reasonable level of success. For example, when the Community College of Denver discovered that a single mother lost welfare benefits in direct proportion to the college's financial aid package and that she would be unable to continue her classes, CCD began work to prevent support from one source from jeopardizing support from another, on the condition that continued good progress was made toward the larger goal of achieving self-sufficiency through training. As CCD discovered, working collaboratively takes time—negotiations around the situation described here took a full year—but ultimately can pay off. But colleges must ask the right questions—first of the students, by caring enough to determine how and if the college, in fact, is being helpful or if it is creating other problems. Then they must work to achieve balanced response and action. The best intentions are strengthened by collaborative efforts, often among entities that have not worked together before to solve problems involving their mutual interests.

Students must be involved in a larger sense with the college—in both coursework and the college's extracurricular activities. It is that "fit" with the college, that sense of connectedness, that is critical to any student's deciding to stay (Tinto 1987). Ernest Boyer, former president of the Carnegie Foundation for the Advancement of Teaching, made this observation about what he had learned in his many visits to American high schools:

> I'm impressed that one of the most fundamental pathologies among the young people in our culture is their sense of disconnectedness—their feeling that they do not belong, they do not fit, and there is no defined purpose in their lives. How can one go dead at such an early age? I've been in high schools where it seems to me that many students drop out because no one noticed that they had dropped in. (Boyer 1992, 4)

Colleges that actively engage all students in the life of the institution from the moment they come in until they depart will improve their chances with at-risk students as well.

Recommendation 5: Abolish voluntary placement in remedial courses. Voluntary placement in remedial courses when assessment data indicate that basic skill instruction is critical to a student's successful future performance is a major shortcoming in what otherwise may be well-planned programs. Colleges that value assessment need to ask themselves why they make so much effort to assess students' academic skills—in fact, making assessment mandatory—and then leave the decision to enroll in remedial courses in the hands of the unprepared students.

Allowing students to enroll in continuing education or avocational courses after they have been tested but before they have done remedial work can be justified. However, information from community colleges that make assessment and placement mandatory, together with data reporting the performance of all students taking remedial work, suggests that remediation correlates with improved performance over the rest of the college experience.

Colleges in states that require assessment and placement report that student retention and success levels improved when mandatory policies were enforced. Many educators and legislators have predicted that state requirements for mandatory placement will become more widespread over the next several years.

Critics of mandatory placement argue that motivation plays a major part in success, that no one can rule out test bias, and that adults should be allowed to make their own choices. However, motivation cannot replace missing or inadequate skill development, assessment tests are valid indicators of more serious deficiencies, and adulthood is not a "free pass" to every course in the college curriculum. Prerequisites for college-level work have been powerful gatekeepers in the past, even for courses in which there has been little or no evidence that the prerequisite experience or skill is critical to classroom success. Finally, critics of mandatory placement who cite students who decline remedial work but are successful in regular college courses should question the rigor of college-level courses in which underprepared students can succeed. On a more positive note, colleges might seriously consider the benefit that tutors, learning assistance centers, and other support services have for all students, especially those who are at risk.

Recommendation 6: Create a more seamless web. Critics who point to remedial education in college as evidence of a dysfunctional public education system are also quick to criticize higher education's refusal to challenge the educational system's poor performance. Placing blame requires too much time and energy, and it should be put aside in the interest of using time more wisely. A plan for improving student performance, developed and implemented by colleges in partnership with public schools, elementary through high school, has the greatest potential for achieving college readiness for first-time students; such a plan will take time. Community college leaders argue that such collaboration is critical to the ultimate goal of eliminating the need for remedial education as we know it now in higher education. "If the community college is to lead transformation of education in the community toward a policy of lifelong learning, there are two stages of community education critical to this process that invite creative partnerships—early childhood education and secondary education" (Gleazer 1998).

> Attitudes towards the sort of learning that will continue throughout life are formed in the family but also, more broadly, at the stage of basic education (which includes, in particular, preprimary and primary schooling): it is there that the spark of creativity may either spring into life or be extinguished, and that access to knowledge may or may not become a reality. This is the time when we all acquire the instruments for the future development of

> our faculties of reason and imagination, our judgement and sense of responsibility, when we learn to be inquisitive about the world around us. (DeLors 1996, 115)

The community college's relative proximity to secondary education would make that segment of the public education system a more likely partner; but although various commissions over the years have urged closer ties between the two, only a few institutions have responded. Instead, "we have tended to give more attention to where our students are going than to where they have been" (Gleazer 1998).

> In general . . . if . . . one had to point to an emergency situation, it would be to secondary education that we would turn our attention, given that the fate of millions of boys and girls is decided between the time they leave primary school and the time they either start work or go on to higher education. This is where the crunch comes in our education systems, either because those systems are too elitist or because they fail to come to terms with massive enrollments because of inertia and total inability to adapt. At a time when these young people are struggling with the problems of adolescence, when they feel, in a sense, mature but are in fact still immature, when instead of being carefree they are worried about their future, the important thing is to provide them with places where they can learn and discover, to give them the wherewithal to think about their future and prepare for it, and to offer them a choice of pathways suited to their abilities. It is also important to ensure that avenues ahead of them are not blocked and that *remedial action and in-course correction of their educational careers are at all times possible* [italics added]. (DeLors 1996, 32)

Various current studies of efforts to help secondary students better prepare themselves for college are being conducted by secondary school districts. One such study, *Charting the Right Course,* published in 1998 by ACT, Inc., and the Council of the Great City Schools, drew 15 recommendations and promising practices from its investigation; the following extracts from these recommendations should be of particular interest to all those concerned with higher education:

- Encourage all students to take more than the core academic preparation.
- Encourage school administrators to seek additional funding from external agencies or foundations to increase the number of students from underrepresented groups who enroll in and succeed in mathematics and science courses. Students of color continue to attain lower achievement levels than their counterparts. Special efforts should be made to ensure that these students have the same opportunity to learn as other students.
- Establish a close working relationship between the high school and nearby postsecondary institutions. Students who are involved in internship programs, shadowing experiences, and other relevant experiences are better prepared to enter postsecondary education.
- Offer test preparation classes before, during and/or after school. Good test preparation courses can be helpful, although nothing can substitute for a student taking the correct course sequence.
- Ensure that each school has a plan for improving its academic performance. All students benefit when a school has a clear mission.
- Prepare an individual education plan with academic goals for each student upon entrance to high school.
- Seek funding to pay for students to take college entrance exams, so that all students, regardless of family income, have an equal opportunity to take the examination. Both the ACT Assessment and the SAT offer waivers for students who need financial support.

A recent study of at-risk students who graduated from high school and enrolled in college revealed that parents play an influential role in teens enrolling in postsecondary education but not in their choice of colleges; that having friends with college plans doubled the odds of students enrolling in some college over not enrolling at all; and that associating with friends who were engaged in learning activities increased the chances for enrolling. However, neither parental influence nor having friends with college plans increased students' odds of enrolling in college immediately after graduation or of continuing full time after enrollment. Receiving help from teachers or school staff in the college application process or with financial aid sources and forms appeared to increase the odds for enrollment. "In the end, this study showed that intervention, whether on the part of the parents or the school, played a positive role in helping moderate- to high-risk students make the transition from high school to college" (Horn, Chen, and MPR Associates 1998, 25–27).

Community colleges must do a better job of encouraging such strategies at the high school level and then be prepared to assume responsibility for appropriate next-step interventions in college. There is considerable evidence available from other transition studies—both high school to college and community college to four-year institution—that direct interventions to provide support and direction should not be abandoned by one institution before they are assumed by another. Collaboration and strong linking mechanisms are critical to successful transition.

Recommendation 7: Strengthen the web with other partnerships. The seamless web is expandable and can embrace multiple partners who share the interest of improving student performance at all educational levels. Currently, more than 35 community colleges across the country are partnering with the Voyager Expanded Learning Initiative to offer a prepackaged program, "Kids on Campus" (often referred to as "College for Kids" or "Kiddie College") for continuing education during the summer. Voyager works in partnership with public school districts nationwide to improve student academic performance and to involve government agencies, nonprofit organizations, and major corporations in mobilizing community resources. Colleges can access additional resources, such as content set in real-world applications, through Voyager's partnerships with the Smithsonian Institution, NASA, and the Discovery Channel. Classes are taught on school district property or on the college campus. Reports are that stronger relationships are being established between districts and colleges; moreover, as a result of success with these summer offerings, some of the colleges are adding after-school programs, and others are planning to offer gifted-and-talented programs as well (Bumphus 1998).

Colleges are not only partnering with businesses to positively affect the future of children and young adults, they are looking to private businesses with a history of helping students become more successful academically. Kaplan Educational Centers, best known for its SAT-preparation courses, and Sylvan Learning Systems, a tutoring company, are two of the companies that offer remedial programs to community colleges.

"Remedial education is becoming big business" (Gose 1997). These companies design, oversee, and otherwise partner with colleges to teach remedial courses; they promise to produce more students who are ready for college-level courses in less time and with better skills than the colleges can. In essence, they promise to accelerate the remedial process, save college funds, and improve at-risk students' perceptions of college—ultimately increasing future enrollments. The results of these partnerships are mixed; most reports from supporters and critics claim that it is too early to know for sure what results might be achieved. Other colleges, after some experience, report that they can document the money and time saved by the college and the student, and cite improvements in staff and faculty morale.

As private businesses identify a sizable population that they believe can profit by their services, community colleges must determine if they need the help or the competition; but the public's interest in improving student performance eventually will demand that colleges defend their decisions about collaboration. The improved skills and self-esteem that private companies claim they can offer their students will look infinitely better if colleges are unable to improve upon their own track records.

Community colleges must consider the nature of and appropriate limits on the company they choose to keep in any new venture. While Rudyard Kipling's notion that "he travels the fastest who travels alone" is no longer an appropriate strategy for success, too many community colleges choose to work in isolation for fear of taking on more than they can manage or assuming more responsibility than they can afford. Investigating other colleges' partnership experiences will help identify opportunities for expanding services and increasing funding.

Conclusions

Mark Twain observed that a good boat captain does not know just one spot in the water well; he knows the shape of the river. Our 20/20 hindsight tells us that most community colleges have wasted their "honeymoon" years with remedial education. They had the luxury of time to "learn the river"—that is, to resolve their differences and clarify their ideologies about remedial education as a major curriculum effort, to establish remedial education policies and programs, to experiment with their own strategies and adapt the most successful strategies of others, and to learn how best to evaluate their performance with at-risk students.

Institutions probably did not recognize that they were in this phase because they were facing many other serious challenges. But current events should be creating a sense of urgency unlike any that community colleges have felt before. Unfortunately, colleges no longer have the luxury of planning a measured response. They are compelled to learn the river's shape by studying the experiences of captains who have ventured farther ahead on the river.

We challenge community colleges to ask themselves certain key questions:

Should we expect no more of ourselves than the current data report about our success with at-risk students? If community colleges are the experts in adult learning, if we are in the best positions to serve our communities because we are of and about them, can we also claim that we really are putting forth our best efforts to be successful with this population and that we really want to make that effort? Current reports indicate that, in good programs, approximately 50 percent of all students complete their remedial work successfully; however, there are no reliable, collective data sources to support this claim. While some colleges may collect retention data in a regular fashion, the majority do not collect or disseminate this information. In fact, during our brief survey, some respondents indicated that their institution's retention data were not available for public dissemination. Most colleges cannot document 50 percent success rates. The rates in Texas and other states are much lower.

However, if colleges *could* document that 50 percent of the students enrolled in remedial courses leave them successfully, we should take nothing away from this success, especially if those who continue do as well or better than students enrolling without major academic deficiencies. The critical question about what happened and what will happen to the other 50 percent is still problematic. Many educators argue that 50 percent is a highly respectable success rate with the at-risk population, further reminding us that many community colleges do not do that well with students who enroll with far fewer or no academic deficiencies.

We contend that losing 50 percent of any population is unacceptable, particularly when colleges cannot explain with certainty how or why the loss occurs. If colleges are to explain these figures without arousing more public ire, they must do a far better job of documenting students' goals (or lack of goals) when they enter college. Documenting student goals will help colleges (1) explain future student behavior that reflects negatively on the college, such as students transferring to a four-year college without completing the associate degree or leaving the college after completing only one course as a job requirement for updating skills, and (2) establish clearer criteria against which to judge how effectively they have worked to achieve these goals.

Such critical questions as these should be part of the larger discussion: How accurate are the percentages that colleges report? Does a college calculate success rates using first-day enrollment totals or figures from later in the semester or quarter, after some students have already departed? Is it possible that numbers documenting successful completion err on the high side? Do we have real data to explain why students were unsuccessful? Once we have our explanations, what are we willing to do about what we have learned? And what happens next to students who are successful, and to those who are not?

With all that community colleges know today about successes with at-risk students, a 50 percent success rate is not high enough. It is possible that sometime in the future, community colleges will have data to prove that it was, in fact, the best that could be done. What we can count on absolutely is that community colleges will have to share their results and justify them to others who will demand to know and who will have the public support and the authority needed to take either corrective or supportive action.

Are community colleges willing to identify the at-risk student population as an opportunity and to embrace improved retention and goal achievement as a potential critical revenue stream? The recent GPRA law governing federal funding agencies and their grantees is a harbinger of things to come. We urge colleges to pay attention to recent legislative discussions and proposed bills to reward colleges with additional funds for every disadvantaged, first-generation-to-college, at-risk student they enroll, and, even more important, with additional funds for students who are retained. Would colleges work more diligently for such rewards? Maybe so, but they would do it by someone else's rules. Are community colleges committed to being "democracy's colleges"? Do they believe so strongly that they can make a difference for themselves and for the country's economic well-being that they are willing to take on this urgent national problem and be the vanguard of an extraordinary national effort?

To date, there is little evidence that community colleges have stepped up to the tasks. We believe that the institutions can do it if they choose to do so and put their creative talents to the effort. Some community colleges are able to document strong progress, and some of their stories of "mission possible" have been included in this document. Whether all community colleges will choose to accept the at-risk student challenge is another story. Many are still listening to strong voices who argue in favor of raising scores on assessment tests in order to reduce the numbers of at-risk students coming to their doors; that money is better spent on programs for more "worthy" students and for a return to more traditional times; and that it is time to reconsider the open-door tradition.

What we know is that an impatient audience is ready to hear a better story than they are hearing now. If community colleges do not tell it, someone else will. The options are becoming more limited, but there is still time left to craft a tale of success. We contend that it *should be* our story to tell. Community colleges should continue making good on the promises of the open door!

Bibliography

ACT, Inc., and the Council of the Great City Schools. 1998. *Charting the Right Course: A Report on Urban Student Achievement and Course-Taking.* Washington, D.C.: Council of the Great City Schools.

Adelman, C. 1998. "The Kiss of Death? An Alternative View of College Remediation." *Cross Talk* 6 (3): 11.

Astin, A. W. 1985. *Achieving Education Excellence: A Critical Assessment of Priorities and Practices in Higher Education.* San Francisco: Jossey-Bass.

———. 1998. "Remedial Education and Civic Responsibility." *CrossTalk* 6 (3): 12–13.

Blanchette, C. M. 1997. *Student Financial Aid: Federal Aid Awarded to Students Taking Remedial Courses.* Washington D.C.: United States General Accounting Office (GAO/HEHS-97-142) (August).

Bok, D. 1979. "Beyond the Ivory Tower." *Town and Country* (May): 28–31.

Boyer, E. L. 1992. "Curriculum, Culture, and Social Cohesion." *Celebrations* (November).

Boylan, H. R., and B. S. Bonham. 1992. "The Impact of Developmental Education Programs." *Research in Developmental Education* 9 (5).

Boyle, M. R. 1990. "Projections of Changing Labor Force Skill Mix Through the Year 2000." *Economic Development Review* (Winter): 7–9.

Brock, W. E. 1993. "Chairman's Preface." In *An American Imperative: Higher Expectations for Higher Education,* The Wingspread Group on Higher Education. Milwaukee, Wis.: The Johnson Foundation.

Bumphus, W. 1998. "With Community Colleges' Help, Voyager Program Expands Learning Opportunities for Children." *Community College Journal* 68 (June/July): 22–24.

Comer, J. P. 1996. "Waiting for a Miracle." *School Development Program Newsline* (Fall): 1–3, 6–8.

Cross, K. P. 1971. *Beyond the Open Door.* San Francisco: Jossey-Bass.

Dana Center. 1998. *Increasing Enrollment, Retention, and Graduation in Texas Public Higher Education.* Austin, Tex.: The University of Texas at Austin.

DeLors, J. 1996. *Learning: The Treasure Within.* Report to UNESCO of the International Commission on Education for the Twenty-First Century. Paris: UNESCO.

"Demonstrating Results: An Introduction to the Government Performance and Results Act." 1998. Higher Education Programs, Office of Postsecondary Education. Washington, D.C.: U.S. Department of Education.

Fallon, J. E. 1996. "The Impact of Immigration on U.S. Demographics." *The Journal of Social, Political and Economic Studies* 21 (Summer).

Gleazer, E. J., ed. 1963. *American Junior Colleges.* 6th ed. Washington, D.C.: American Council on Education.

———. 1998. Personal correspondence (September).

Gose, B. 1997. "Tutoring Companies Take Over Remedial Teaching at Some Colleges: Can Kaplan and Sylvan Help Students Erase Educational Deficiencies More Quickly?" *The Chronicle of Higher Education* (19 September): A44–A45.

Grastie, K. 1998a. "Greenville Technical College and Kaplan Learning Services: A Joint Partnership for Creating Successful Innovations in Developmental Studies." In *Developmental Education: A Twenty-First Century Social and Economic Imperative,* R. H. McCabe and P. R. Day Jr., 59–65. Mission Viejo, Calif.: League for Innovation in the Community College and The College Board.

———. 1998b. Personal correspondence (October).

Harman, D. 1987. *Illiteracy: A National Dilemma.* New York: Cambridge.

Hartle, T. W., and J. E. King. 1997. "The End of Equal Opportunity in Higher Education?" *The College Board Review* 181 (July): 8–15.

Hodgkinson, H. 1997. "Diversity Comes in All Sizes and Shapes." *School Business Affairs* (April).

Horn, L. J., X. Chen, and MPR Associates. 1998. *Toward Resiliency: At-Risk Students Who Make It to College.* Washington, D.C.: U.S. Department of Education, Office of Educational Research and Improvement (May).

Immerwahr, J., J. Johnson, and A. Kernan-Schloss. 1991. *Cross Talk: The Public, the Experts, and Competitiveness.* Washington, D.C.: The Business–Higher Education Forum and the Public Agenda Foundation (February).

Jackson, G. A. 1988. "Did College Choice Change During the 1970s?" *Economics of Education Review* 7 (1): 15–17.

Locksley, N. 1998. "A Trustee Looks at Remedial/Developmental Education." *Trustee* Quarterly 1: 13–15.

Manno, B. V. 1995. "Remedial Education: Replacing the Double Standard with Real Standards." *Change* 27 (May/June): 47–49.

McCabe, R. H. 1995. *Remedial Education in Florida's Community Colleges: Cost-Effective for Floridians.* Miami, Fla.: Miami-Dade Community College Foundation.

McCabe, R. H., and P. R. Day Jr. 1998. *Developmental Education: A Twenty-First Century Social and Economic Imperative.* Mission Viejo, Calif.: League for Innovation in the Community College and The College Board.

McClenney, B. N., and R. M. Flores. 1998. "Community College of Denver Developmental Education." In *Developmental Education: A Twenty-First Century Social and Economic Imperative,* R. H. McCabe and P. R. Day Jr., 45–52. Mission Viejo, Calif.: League for Innovation in the Community College and The College Board.

McClenney, K. M. 1998. "Community Colleges Perched at the Millennium: Perspectives on Innovation, Transformation, and Tomorrow." *Leadership Abstracts* 11 (8).

McMillan, J. 1997. "Remedial Education Programs in Texas Face Uncertain Future." *The Chronicle of Higher Education* (17 January): A35.

Milliron, M. D., and E. R. Leach. 1998. "Community Colleges Winning through Innovation: Taking on the Changes and Choices of Leadership in the Twenty-First Century." *Leadership Abstracts*, Special Edition.

Moloney, W. 1996. "Reading at the 8th Grade Level—in College." *Fayetteville Observer-Times* (11 December): 11A.

National Association of Manufacturers. 1997. *The Skilled Workforce Shortage: A Growing Challenge to the Future Competitiveness of American Manufacturing.* Washington, D.C.: National Association of Manufacturers (November).

National Center for Education Statistics (NCES). 1995. *Profile of Undergraduates in U.S. Postsecondary Education Institutions*, 1992–1993. Washington, D.C.: U.S. Department of Education, Office of Educational Research and Improvement.

———. 1996. *Remedial Education at Higher Education Institutions in Fall 1995.* Washington, D.C.: U.S. Department of Education, Office of Educational Research and Improvement.

National Center on Education and the Economy. 1990. *America's Choice: High Skills or Low Wages!* Rochester, N.Y.: National Center on Education and the Economy.

Northcutt, N., et al. 1975. *Adult Functional Competency: A Summary.* Austin, Tex.: The University of Texas Division of Extension.

Osborne, J. W. 1997. "Identification with Academics and Academic Success among Community College Students." *Community College Review*, Spring 25 (1): 59–67.

Parker, A. E., Jr., and S. Ratliff. 1998. "Paying for Public Higher Education Twice: Remediation in Texas Public Higher Education." San Antonio, Tex.: Texas Public Policy Foundation.

Pogrow, S. 1998. "What Is an Exemplary Program, and Why Should Anyone Care? A Reaction to Slavin & Klein." *Education Researcher* 27 (October): 22–28.

Preston, S. H. 1996. "Children Will Pay. Demography's Crystal Ball Shows that 21st Century America Will Be Older, Wiser and More Ethnically Diverse. But Kids Face Trouble." *New York Times Magazine* (29 September).

"Ready or Not: California Plans to Cut Down Remedial Courses at Four-Year Colleges." 1995. *The Chronicle of Higher Education* 41 (29) (March): A23.

Reising, B. 1997. "Postsecondary Remediation." *Clearinghouse* 7, no. 4 (March/April): 172–173.

Roueche, J. E. 1968. *Salvage, Redirection, or Custody? Remedial Education in the Community Junior College.* Washington, D.C.: American Association of Community Colleges.

Roueche, J. E., and S. D. Roueche. 1993. *Between a Rock and a Hard Place: The At-Risk Student in the Open-Door College.* Washington, D.C.: Community College Press, American Association of Community Colleges.

———. 1996. "Making Good on the Promises of the Open Door." In *The 21st Century: Investing in Our Students,* eds. P. C. Williamson and A. J. Matonak. Iowa City: American College Testing.

———. 1998. "Dancing as Fast as They Can." *Community College Journal* 68 (April/May): 30–35.

Roueche, J. E., S. D. Roueche, and M. D. Milliron. 1995. *Strangers in Their Own Land: Part-Time Faculty in American Community Colleges.* Washington, D.C.: Community College Press, American Association of Community Colleges.

Shaw, K. M. 1997. "Remedial Education as Ideological Battleground: Emerging Remedial Education Policies in the Community College." *Educational Evaluation and Policy Analysis* 19, no. 3 (Fall): 284–296.

Smith, J. O., and R. A. Price. 1996. *Journal of Developmental Education.* 19, no. 3 (Spring): 2–6.

Smith, T. M., B. A. Young, Y. Bae, S. P. Choy, and N. Alsalam. 1997. *The Condition of Education.* Washington, D.C.: U.S. Department of Education, Office of Educational Research and Improvement, National Center for Education Statistics.

Stitcht, T., and B. McDonald. 1990. *Teach the Mother and Reach the Child: Literacy Across Generations.* Geneva, Switzerland: International Bureau of Education (ED 321 063).

Tinto, V. 1987. *Leaving College: Rethinking the Causes and Cures of Student Attrition.* Chicago: The University of Chicago Press.

Vaughan, G. B. 1985. "Maintaining Open Access and Comprehensiveness." In *Maintaining Institutional Integrity: New Directions for Community Colleges,* ed. D. Puyear, 52: 17–29. San Francisco: Jossey-Bass.

Wattenbarger, J. L., and W. L. Godwin, eds. 1962. *The Community College in the South: Progress and Prospects,* 1962. A report of the Southern States Work Conference, Committee on Education Beyond the High School.

Weissman, J., E. Silk, and C. Bulakowski. 1997. "Assessing Developmental Education Policies." *Research in Higher Education* 38 (2): 187–200.

Wright, S. W. 1998. "The Ill-Prepared and the Ill-Informed: The Story behind the Remediation Feud in New York." *Black Issues in Higher Education* (5 March): 12–15.

Index

About the Authors

John E. Roueche is professor and director of the Community College Leadership Program at The University of Texas at Austin, where he holds the Sid W. Richardson Regents Chair in Community College Leadership. The author of 33 books and more than 150 articles and monographs on educational leadership and teaching effectiveness, Roueche has spoken to more than 1,300 colleges and universities since 1970. He is the recipient of numerous national awards for his research, teaching, services, and overall leadership, including the 1986 National Leadership Award from the American Association of Community Colleges.

Suanne D. Roueche is director of the National Institute for Staff and Organizational Development; editor of *Innovation Abstracts,* NISOD's weekly teaching tips publication; editor of *Linkages,* NISOD's quarterly newsletter; and senior lecturer in the Department of Educational Administration, College of Education, The University of Texas at Austin. The author of more than 13 books and more than 40 articles and book chapters, she is the recipient of numerous national awards, including the 1997 National Leadership Award from the American Association of Community Colleges.